EASY ANTHEMS

General Editor David Willcocks

SSA and organ

OXFORD

D1739635

The Peace of God

John Rutter

MUSIC DEPARTMENT

OXFORD

UNIVERSITY PRESS

The Peace of God

Book of Common Prayer (1662)
based on Philippians 4, v.7

JOHN RUTTER

Also available for mixed voices (E157). An orchestral arrangement for strings is available from the publisher's Hire Library.

Printed in Great Britain

OXFORD UNIVERSITY PRESS, MUSIC DEPARTMENT, GREAT CLARENDON STREET, OXFORD OX2 6DP

know-ledge and love of God, and of his Son Je-sus Christ___ our Lord: The

ALTOS

The

A

peace of God, which pass-eth all un-der-stand-ing,___

peace of God, which pass-eth all un-der-stand-ing,___

keep your hearts and minds, keep your hearts and minds in the

keep your hearts and minds,___ keep you in the

know-ledge and love of God, and of his Son Je-sus Christ our

know-ledge and love of God, and of his Son Je-sus Christ our

Lord: and the bless-ing of God Al - migh - ty,

Lord: and the bless-ing of God Al - migh - ty,

the Fa - ther, the Son, and the Ho - ly Ghost, be a-

the Fa - ther, the Son, and the Ho - ly Ghost, be a-

40

S.1 -mongst you,_____ be a-mongst you,_____ be a-

S.2 -mongst you,_____ be a-mongst you,_____ be a-

A. -mongst you,_____ be a-mongst you, a-mongst you, be a-

cresc. *mp* *cresc.* *mf*

44

-mongst you and re-main with you al - ways._____

-mongst you and re-main with you al - - - ways._____

-mongst you and re-main with you al - ways._____

cresc. *f*

Reproduced and printed by
Halstan & Co. Ltd., Amersham, Bucks., England

W110   **The Peace of God (S.S.A.)** RUTTER

ISBN 0-19-342609-9

9 780193 426092